Go Viral

The Ultimate Guide to Owning Social Media

Riley Anderson

Copyright © 2024 Riley Anderson

All rights reserved.

DEDICATION

To all those who strive for fulfillment in their careers,

This book is dedicated to you.

May its pages offer guidance, inspiration, and support

as you navigate the twists and turns of your professional journey.

Your dedication to finding meaning and satisfaction in your work

inspires us all to reach for our highest aspirations.

May you find fulfillment, purpose, and joy

in every step you take towards your dreams.

This is for you.

CONTENTS

ACKNOWLEDGMENTS..1
CHAPTER 1..1
Demystifying Social Media Marketing..1
    Understanding the Social Media Landscape..............................1
    Defining Your Social Media Goals...3
    Building Your Social Media Foundation....................................4
CHAPTER 2..7
Content is King (and Queen): Content Strategy...........................7
    Content Pillars and Calendars: The Backbone of Consistency...7
    Crafting Engaging Content: The Art of Captivating Your Audience..9
    Staying Ahead of the Curve: Adaptation is Key.......................10
CHAPTER 3..13
The Power of Community Building: Cultivating Connections in the Digital Age...13
    Fostering Engagement: The Art of Two-Way Communication 13
    Building Relationships with Influencers: Expanding Your Reach 14
    Community Management Strategies: Nurturing a Positive Online Space..16
CHAPTER 4..18
Paid Advertising for Maximum Impact: Supercharge Your Reach. 18
    Understanding Paid Social Media Advertising: A World of Options...18
    Campaign Targeting and Optimization: Reaching the Right Audience, Right Now..20
    Tracking and Analyzing Paid Ads: Measuring Success for Informed Decisions..21
CHAPTER 5..24
Mastering Visual Storytelling: Captivate Your Audience with Stunning Visuals...24

    The Importance of Visual Content: Seeing is Believing............ 24
    Creating High-Quality Visuals: Unleash Your Inner Designer. 26
    Leveraging Visual Content for Different Platforms:
    Tailor-Made for Success... 28

CHAPTER 6.. 30

Social Media for Lead Generation and Sales: Turning Engagement into Customers.. 30

    Crafting Effective Lead Capture Forms: The Gateway to
    Conversion.. 30

    Nurturing Leads through Social Media: Building Trust and
    Relationships.. 32

    Converting Leads into Paying Customers: The Final Push....... 33

CHAPTER 7.. 36

Building a Loyal Brand Community: Cultivating Devoted Fans in the Digital Age.. 36

    The Importance of Brand Advocacy: Your Biggest Cheerleaders 36

    Encouraging User-Generated Content: Amplify Your Brand
    Story.. 38

    Building Brand Loyalty through Social Listening: A Listening
    Ear... 40

CHAPTER 8.. 42

Analytics and Measuring Success: Decoding the Data for Social Media Domination... 42

    Key Social Media Metrics: The Numbers that Matter................ 42

    Utilizing Social Media Analytics Tools: Unveiling Hidden
    Insights.. 44

    A/B Testing and Optimization: The Continuous Improvement
    Cycle.. 46

CHAPTER 9.. 48

Staying Ahead of the Curve: Social Media Trends in a Dynamic Landscape... 48

    Emerging Social Media Platforms: The Next Big Thing?......... 48

    The Rise of Social Commerce: Shopping Made Easy................ 49

    Future-Proofing Your Social Media Strategy: A Long-Term

  Vision 50
CHAPTER 10 .... **53**
Conclusion: Mastering Social Media - A Journey of Dedication and Continuous Growth **53**
  The Importance of Consistency: Building Momentum for Long-Term Success 53
  Celebrate Your Wins and Learn from Losses: Tracking Progress for Informed Decisions 55
  Embrace the Journey: The Evolving World of Social Media 56
Bonus Chapter **58**
Social Media Management Tools and Resources - Your All-in-One Toolkit for Success **58**
  Social Media Management Tools: 58
  Design Resources: 60
  Stock Photo and Video Websites: 61
  Social Listening Platforms: 62
ABOUT THE AUTHOR **64**

ACKNOWLEDGMENTS

I would like to express my heartfelt gratitude to everyone who contributed to the creation of this book.

First and foremost, I am deeply thankful to my family for their unwavering support, patience, and encouragement throughout this journey. Your belief in me has been a constant source of strength.

I extend my sincere appreciation to my friends and colleagues who provided valuable insights, feedback, and encouragement along the way. Your perspectives enriched this project in ways I could never have imagined.

I am grateful to the mentors and educators who have guided and inspired me with their wisdom and expertise. Your mentorship has been instrumental in shaping my understanding of career fulfillment.

A special thank you to the readers who have embraced this book. Your curiosity and eagerness to learn motivate me to continue sharing knowledge and insights.

Lastly, I want to acknowledge the countless individuals who have shared their stories, experiences, and expertise in the field of career development. Your collective wisdom has laid the foundation for this work, and I am deeply grateful for your contributions.

Go Viral

Thank you all for being part of this journey.

CHAPTER 1

Demystifying Social Media Marketing

Welcome to the exciting world of social media marketing! In this chapter, we'll shed light on the ever-evolving social media landscape, guide you through defining your goals, and help you build a solid foundation for your brand's online presence.

Understanding the Social Media Landscape

Imagine a vast digital town square, bustling with conversations, trends, and communities. That's the essence of social media! Here, you'll find a diverse range of platforms, each catering to specific audiences and offering unique functionalities. Let's explore some of the major players:

- **Facebook:** The granddaddy of social media,

Facebook boasts a massive user base across all demographics. It's ideal for brand storytelling, building communities, and driving website traffic.

- **Instagram:** A visually-driven platform, Instagram thrives on high-quality photos and videos. It's perfect for showcasing products, sharing behind-the-scenes glimpses, and connecting with a younger audience.
- **Twitter:** Known for its fast-paced nature and real-time updates, Twitter excels at live event coverage, customer service interactions, and sharing bite-sized news and announcements.
- **LinkedIn:** The professional networking platform, LinkedIn is a goldmine for B2B (business-to-business) marketing. It allows you to connect with industry professionals, promote thought leadership content, and establish your brand as an authority in your field.
- **YouTube:** The world's second-largest search engine (after Google), YouTube reigns supreme for video content. Share educational tutorials, product

demonstrations, or brand stories to capture attention and build trust.

Understanding the unique strengths and target demographics of each platform is crucial. By identifying which platforms resonate best with your audience, you can tailor your content and strategies for maximum impact.

Defining Your Social Media Goals

Social media marketing without clear goals is like driving without a destination. Before diving in, take a step back and ask yourself: What do you want to achieve with your social media presence?

Here's where the SMART goal framework comes in. It ensures your goals are:

- **Specific:** Clearly define what you want to accomplish. Do you aim to increase brand awareness, generate leads, or boost website traffic?
- **Measurable:** Establish metrics to track your

progress. This could involve follower growth, engagement rates (likes, comments, shares), or website clicks.

- **Achievable:** Set realistic goals that are attainable with your resources and budget.
- **Relevant:** Ensure your goals align with your overall marketing strategy and business objectives.
- **Time-Bound:** Assign a specific timeframe for achieving your goals. This creates a sense of urgency and helps you measure progress.

For example, instead of a vague goal like "get more popular on social media," a SMART goal might be: "Increase brand awareness on Instagram by 20% within the next quarter, measured by follower growth and engagement rate."

Building Your Social Media Foundation

With your goals in mind, it's time to lay the groundwork for your social media success. Here's what you need to focus on:

- **Compelling Social Media Profiles:** Craft impactful profiles that tell your brand story and attract potential followers. Optimize your bio with relevant keywords, include a captivating cover photo, and ensure your contact information is readily available.
- **Brand Consistency:** Maintain a consistent visual identity across all platforms. Use the same logos, color schemes, and fonts to create a recognizable brand image. This fosters trust and strengthens brand recognition.
- **Search Optimization:** Optimize your profiles for search engines by including relevant keywords in your bios and descriptions. This helps potential customers discover your brand when they search for related terms.

By understanding the social media landscape, defining clear goals, and building a strong foundation, you've taken the first crucial steps towards social media marketing mastery. Now, let's move on to crafting engaging content that truly resonates with your audience!

CHAPTER 2

CONTENT IS KING (AND QUEEN): CONTENT STRATEGY

In the realm of social media marketing, content reigns supreme. It's the currency that attracts attention, fuels engagement, and ultimately drives results.

Content Pillars and Calendars: The Backbone of Consistency

Imagine your social media presence as a captivating story. Content pillars are the core themes that define your narrative. These themes should resonate with your target audience and align with your brand identity. Here are some examples:

- **Industry Insights:** Share valuable knowledge and expertise to establish your brand as a thought leader.
- **Product or Service Focus:** Showcase the benefits

and features of your offerings through engaging content.

- **Behind-the-Scenes Glimpses:** Offer a peek into your company culture, team, and values to foster stronger connections with your audience.
- **Customer Testimonials:** Let your satisfied customers do the talking by featuring positive reviews and success stories.

Once you've identified your content pillars, it's time to create a content calendar. This roadmap ensures consistent posting and keeps your social media presence active. A well-organized calendar helps you:

- **Plan your content in advance:** Batch-create content to save time and maintain a steady flow of posts.
- **Schedule posts strategically:** Consider factors like time zones and peak engagement times for each platform.
- **Maintain variety:** Integrate different content formats like text posts, images, videos, and live

streams to keep your audience engaged.

- **Collaborate effectively:** Share the calendar with your team to ensure everyone is on the same page and deadlines are met.

Pro Tip: Utilize free or paid social media management tools to simplify content scheduling and streamline your workflow.

Crafting Engaging Content: The Art of Captivating Your Audience

Now that your content pillars and calendar are in place, let's explore the different formats that can bring your social media strategy to life:

- **Text Posts:** Short, informative, and thought-provoking text posts can spark conversations, share news, and announce promotions. Utilize relevant hashtags to increase discoverability.

- **Images:** Eye-catching visuals are a powerful way to grab attention and tell stories. Use high-quality photos, infographics, and memes that resonate with your target audience.
- **Videos:** From short snippets to in-depth tutorials, videos are highly engaging and can showcase your brand personality effectively. Leverage platforms like YouTube and Instagram Reels to tap into the power of video content.
- **Live Streams:** Offer real-time interaction with your audience through live Q&A sessions, product demonstrations, or behind-the-scenes glimpses.

Remember: Content optimization is key! Tailor your content format and message to each platform's specific functionalities and user base. For instance, keep Instagram captions concise and visually compelling, while LinkedIn allows for longer-form, informative content.

Staying Ahead of the Curve: Adaptation is Key

The social media landscape is dynamic, and trends evolve rapidly. Here's how to ensure your content strategy stays fresh and relevant:

- **Embrace Trending Topics:** Keep your finger on the pulse of what's trending on social media. Incorporate trending topics and hashtags into your content strategy to tap into existing conversations and expand your reach.
- **Leverage User-Generated Content (UGC):** Empower your audience to become brand advocates by encouraging them to create and share content related to your brand. This fosters a sense of community and authenticity.
- **Data-Driven Decisions:** Analytics are your allies! Monitor social media metrics like engagement rates and reach to understand what content resonates with your audience. Adapt your strategy based on data insights to continuously improve performance.
- **Embrace Feedback:** Pay attention to audience

comments and feedback. Use this valuable input to refine your content and ensure it aligns with their interests.

By consistently creating high-quality content that resonates with your audience, adapts to trends, and leverages data, you'll establish yourself as a thought leader and cultivate a loyal following on social media.

CHAPTER 3

THE POWER OF COMMUNITY BUILDING: CULTIVATING CONNECTIONS IN THE DIGITAL AGE

Social media isn't just about broadcasting messages; it's about fostering genuine connections and building a thriving community around your brand.

Fostering Engagement: The Art of Two-Way Communication

Engagement is the lifeblood of any successful social media community. It's about fostering two-way communication, where your audience feels heard and valued. Here are some tactics to keep your audience engaged:

- **Encourage Conversations:** Ask open-ended questions, respond to comments thoughtfully, and participate in relevant online discussions. This creates a sense of interaction and encourages your audience to actively participate.

- **Respond Promptly:** Show your audience you care by responding to comments and messages as quickly as possible. This builds trust and demonstrates your commitment to customer service.
- **Run Interactive Campaigns:** Spark excitement and interaction through engaging campaigns like polls, contests, and quizzes. This not only encourages participation but also helps you gather valuable insights about your audience's interests.

By prioritizing engagement, you cultivate a loyal community invested in your brand and more receptive to your messages.

Building Relationships with Influencers: Expanding Your Reach

Influencers are individuals with established credibility and a dedicated following within a specific niche. Partnering with the right influencers can significantly amplify your brand's reach and connect you with a highly targeted audience. Here's how to leverage influencer marketing effectively:

- **Identify Relevant Influencers:** Focus on quality over quantity. Seek influencers who align with your brand values, target audience, and content style. Research platforms like Instagram, YouTube, and relevant industry blogs to find potential partners.
- **Collaborate on Content Creation:** Work with influencers to develop creative content that resonates with their audience and promotes your brand. This could involve sponsored posts, product reviews, co-hosted live streams, or participation in influencer marketing campaigns.
- **Leverage Their Reach:** Benefit from the influencer's established audience base to expand your reach and brand awareness. Remember, the goal isn't just about gaining followers but also about

reaching a highly relevant and engaged audience.

Pro Tip: Focus on building genuine relationships with influencers rather than simply transactional collaborations. Transparency and mutual benefit are key for successful influencer partnerships.

Community Management Strategies: Nurturing a Positive Online Space

Building a thriving community requires proactive management. Here's how to ensure your online space fosters positive interactions and reflects well on your brand:

- **Establish Community Guidelines:** Set clear expectations for acceptable behavior within your community. Outline guidelines regarding respectful communication, spam prevention, and consequences for violating the rules.
- **Address Negativity Promptly:** Don't shy away

from negative feedback. Address concerns professionally, listen to the dissatisfaction, and offer solutions where possible. Addressing negativity head-on demonstrates your commitment to customer satisfaction and prevents negativity from escalating.

- **Foster a Positive Brand Image:** Cultivate a welcoming and positive environment by celebrating successes, highlighting user-generated content, and showcasing positive customer experiences. This fosters loyalty and encourages further positive interactions within the community.

By implementing effective community management strategies, you create a space where your audience feels valued and empowered to interact with each other and your brand in a positive and constructive way.

CHAPTER 4

Paid Advertising for Maximum Impact: Supercharge Your Reach

While organic social media marketing is essential, paid advertising unlocks an incredible potential to amplify your reach, target specific audiences, and achieve your marketing goals with laser precision.

Understanding Paid Social Media Advertising: A World of Options

Paid social media advertising offers a diverse range of options to suit your specific needs. Here's a breakdown of some key advertising formats:

- **Targeted Ads:** These highly customizable ads reach a specific audience based on demographics (age, location, income), interests (hobbies, passions), and behaviors (online purchases, website visits). This laser targeting ensures your message reaches the most relevant users, maximizing the effectiveness of your ad spend.

- **Boosted Posts:** Give your existing organic content an extra push with boosted posts. By allocating a budget, you can increase the reach and visibility of a specific post to a wider audience within your chosen demographics.

Platform Variations: Each social media platform offers its own unique advertising options. Familiarize yourself with the specific ad formats and targeting capabilities available on platforms like Facebook Ads Manager, Twitter Ads, and LinkedIn Campaign Manager.

Campaign Objectives: Before diving in, define your clear campaign objectives. Do you aim to increase brand awareness, drive website traffic, generate leads, or boost sales? Aligning your ad strategy with your objectives ensures you're measuring the right metrics and optimizing for success.

Campaign Targeting and Optimization: Reaching the Right Audience, Right Now

The power of paid social media advertising lies in its precise targeting capabilities. Here's how to create targeted audiences that maximize your ROI:

- **Demographic Targeting:** Reach users based on factors like age, gender, location, income, and education level. This allows you to tailor your message to resonate with specific demographics relevant to your product or service.
- **Interest Targeting:** Target users based on their interests, hobbies, and online activities. Leverage social media platform data on browsing behavior and past interactions to reach users who are genuinely interested in what you offer.
- **Behavioral Targeting:** Go beyond demographics and interests by targeting users based on their past

actions. This could include website visits, app downloads, or previous purchases. It allows you to reach users who are already familiar with your brand or have demonstrated buying intent.

Lookalike Audiences: Leverage the power of lookalike audiences. These are audiences created by social media platforms that resemble your existing customer base or website visitors. This allows you to target users with similar characteristics, increasing the likelihood of successful conversions.

Campaign Optimization is Key: Don't set your ads and forget them! Regularly monitor your campaigns' performance and make adjustments based on data insights. A/B test different ad creatives, audiences, and budgets to identify the most effective strategies for achieving your goals.

Tracking and Analyzing Paid Ads: Measuring Success for Informed Decisions

Data is your best friend in paid social media advertising. By tracking key metrics, you can understand how your campaigns are performing and make data-driven decisions to optimize them. Here are some essential metrics to focus on:

- **Impressions:** The number of times your ad is displayed on users' screens.
- **Clicks:** The number of times users click on your ad, indicating their interest in learning more.
- **Conversions:** The number of users who complete a desired action, such as making a purchase, signing up for a newsletter, or downloading an app.
- **Cost per Click (CPC):** The average cost you incur each time someone clicks on your ad.
- **Return on Investment (ROI):** The net profit you generate from your ad spend.

By analyzing these metrics, you can determine the effectiveness of your campaigns, identify areas for improvement, and optimize your budget allocation to maximize your return on investment.

Utilize Built-in Analytics Tools: Most social media platforms offer robust built-in analytics tools that provide valuable insights into your ad campaign performance. Utilize these tools to track key metrics and identify trends.

Consider Additional Analytics Software: For deeper insights and advanced campaign management functionalities, consider investing in additional social media analytics software. These tools can offer detailed reporting, competitor analysis, and budget optimization recommendations.

Paid social media advertising, when strategically implemented and meticulously tracked, can be a powerful tool for achieving your marketing goals. By understanding the advertising options, targeting effectively, and analyzing data to optimize your campaigns, you can unlock new levels of reach, engagement, and ultimately, success in the social media landscape.

CHAPTER 5

MASTERING VISUAL STORYTELLING: CAPTIVATE YOUR AUDIENCE WITH STUNNING VISUALS

In the age of social media, attention spans are shorter than ever. Visuals are the language that grabs attention instantly, ignites emotions, and tells your brand story in a captivating way.

The Importance of Visual Content: Seeing is Believing

Visual content reigns supreme in the social media landscape. Here's why incorporating captivating visuals is essential:

- **Increased Engagement:** Eye-catching visuals like infographics, product photos, and creative videos instantly grab attention and encourage users to stop scrolling. Engaging visuals can significantly increase likes, comments, and shares, boosting your overall reach and engagement.

- **Enhanced Brand Storytelling:** Visuals have the power to evoke emotions and tell your brand story in a compelling way. A well-crafted image or video can communicate complex messages more effectively than text alone, fostering a deeper connection with your audience.

- **Improved Brand Recognition:** Visually consistent content across your social media platforms reinforces your brand identity and makes you instantly recognizable. This builds trust and fosters brand loyalty among your audience.

The Power of Different Visual Formats: Explore the diverse range of visual content options at your disposal:

- **Infographics:** Transform complex data into visually appealing and easily digestible snapshots of information.

- **Product Photos:** Showcase your products in a

high-quality and enticing manner, highlighting key features and benefits.

- **Creative Video Content:** Leverage the power of video to tell stories, showcase product demonstrations, or offer behind-the-scenes glimpses into your brand.
- **User-Generated Content (UGC):** Feature photos and videos created by your audience to foster a sense of community and authenticity.

Remember: Visuals are not just decorative elements; they are a strategic tool to achieve your social media goals.

Creating High-Quality Visuals: Unleash Your Inner Designer

Even without a professional design background, you can create compelling visuals for your social media presence. Here are some resources and tips to get you started:

- **Free and Paid Design Tools:** Utilize free online

design tools like Canva or Piktochart to create stunning visuals with user-friendly templates and drag-and-drop functionality. For more advanced features, consider paid design software like Adobe Photoshop or Affinity Designer.

- **Learn Basic Design Principles:** Grasp the fundamentals of design principles like composition, color theory, and typography. Understanding these principles ensures your visuals are visually appealing, balanced, and easy to understand.

- **Stock Photo and Video Resources:** There are numerous websites offering high-quality stock photos and videos at affordable prices (or even for free). Utilize resources like Unsplash, Pexels, or Shutterstock to elevate your visual content without breaking the bank.

Pro Tip: Consistency is key! Maintain a consistent visual style across all your social media platforms to reinforce your brand identity and create a recognizable aesthetic.

Leveraging Visual Content for Different Platforms: Tailor-Made for Success

Each social media platform has its own unique strengths and ideal visual formats. Here's how to tailor your visual content for maximum impact:

- **Facebook:** Facebook allows for a variety of visual formats, including high-resolution images, engaging infographics, and captivating video content (including live streams).
- **Instagram:** A visual powerhouse, Instagram thrives on high-quality photos and creative video formats like Reels and Stories. Utilize captivating visuals to grab attention and tell your brand story in a visually stunning way.
- **Twitter:** While character limits reign supreme on Twitter, eye-catching images and short video clips can significantly boost engagement and retweets.
- **LinkedIn:** Professional and visually appealing infographics and presentations are ideal for

LinkedIn, while high-quality product photos can showcase your services or expertise.

Embrace Platform-Specific Features: Each platform offers unique features for visual content. Leverage features like Instagram Stories, Facebook Live, or Twitter polls to keep your audience engaged and create interactive experiences.

By harnessing the power of captivating visuals, you can transform your social media presence and connect with your audience on a deeper level.

CHAPTER 6

SOCIAL MEDIA FOR LEAD GENERATION AND SALES: TURNING ENGAGEMENT INTO CUSTOMERS

Social media isn't just about building brand awareness; it's a powerful tool for generating leads and nurturing them into loyal customers.

Crafting Effective Lead Capture Forms: The Gateway to Conversion

Lead capture forms are the bridge between online engagement and valuable customer relationships. Here's how to design forms that incentivize users to share their contact information:

- **Offer Valuable Content:** Provide compelling content like ebooks, white papers, webinars, or exclusive discounts in exchange for user information. Ensure the offered content aligns with your target audience's needs and interests.

- **Keep it Short and Sweet:** Don't overwhelm users with too many information fields. Focus on essential details like name, email address, and (if relevant) phone number. Streamlining the process increases the conversion rate.

- **Clear Value Proposition:** Clearly state what users will gain by submitting their information. Highlight the benefits of subscribing to your newsletter, downloading your content, or signing up for a free trial.

- **Visually Appealing Design:** Make your lead capture forms visually appealing and consistent with your overall brand identity. Utilize clear fonts, contrasting colors, and a user-friendly layout to encourage form completion.

A/B Testing is Key: Don't settle for the first draft! Run A/B tests on different lead capture form versions to see which ones convert the best. Analyze data and adjust your design based on results to optimize lead generation.

Nurturing Leads through Social Media: Building Trust and Relationships

Once you've captured leads, the nurturing process begins. Here's how to utilize social media to convert them into paying customers:

- **Provide Valuable Content:** Consistently share valuable content that educates, informs, and resonates with your target audience. This establishes your expertise, fosters trust, and positions you as a thought leader in your industry.

- **Engage with Your Audience:** Don't be a one-way broadcaster! Actively engage with your audience by responding to comments and messages promptly. Participate in relevant conversations and answer their questions to build rapport.

- **Offer Special Promotions:** Leverage social media

to promote exclusive discounts, limited-time offers, and early access to new products. This incentivizes lead conversion and drives sales.

- **Social Proof Matters:** Showcase positive customer testimonials and reviews on your social media platforms. Social proof builds trust and reassures potential customers about the value you offer.

Leverage Social Media Automation Tools: Consider utilizing social media automation tools to schedule content, engage in conversations, and manage your social media presence efficiently, allowing you to dedicate more time to nurturing leads individually.

Converting Leads into Paying Customers: The Final Push

With a strong foundation of valuable content and engagement, it's time to convert your leads into paying customers. Here are some social media strategies to drive sales:

- **Develop Targeted Campaigns:** Run targeted ad campaigns promoting your products or services to users who have already shown interest through lead capture forms or website visits.

- **Retarget Website Visitors:** Utilize retargeting campaigns to remind users who have visited your website but haven't converted yet. This re-engages their interest and encourages them to complete a purchase.

- **Offer Exclusive Deals on Social Media:** Promote special offers and limited-time discounts exclusively through social media platforms. This creates a sense of urgency and incentivizes immediate purchase decisions.

- **Host Social Media Contests and Giveaways:** Create engaging contests and giveaways to generate excitement, increase brand awareness, and capture new leads. Offer desirable prizes related to your product or service.

Measure and Adapt: Track the performance of your social media campaigns for lead generation and sales. Analyze metrics like conversion rates, click-through rates, and customer acquisition costs. Based on the data, refine your strategies to maximize your return on investment (ROI).

Social media offers a unique opportunity to nurture leads and nurture them into loyal customers. By utilizing effective lead capture forms, consistently providing valuable content, and implementing strategic sales campaigns, you can transform your social media audience into a thriving customer base.

CHAPTER 7

Building a Loyal Brand Community: Cultivating Devoted Fans in the Digital Age

Social media transcends mere marketing; it's about forging genuine connections and fostering a community of passionate brand advocates.

The Importance of Brand Advocacy: Your Biggest Cheerleaders

Brand advocates are your most valuable assets. These are passionate fans who love your brand, actively promote it on social media, and recommend it to their networks. Here's why brand advocacy is crucial:

- **Increased Brand Awareness:** Brand advocates organically expand your reach by spreading positive word-of-mouth through their social circles. This significantly increases brand awareness and attracts new customers.

- **Enhanced Brand Credibility:** Positive testimonials and genuine experiences shared by your advocates hold more weight than traditional marketing messages. This builds trust and establishes credibility with potential customers.

- **Boosted Engagement:** Brand advocates actively participate in conversations, share user-generated content, and defend your brand online. This fosters a vibrant community and boosts overall engagement on your social media platforms.

Nurture Your Brand Advocates: Don't take your brand advocates for granted! Recognize and appreciate their contributions by:

- **Featuring User-Generated Content:** Showcase their photos, videos, and testimonials on your social media platforms. This makes them feel valued and encourages others to participate.

- **Exclusive Offers and Incentives:** Consider offering exclusive discounts or early access to new products to your loyal supporters. This shows your appreciation and strengthens their connection to your brand.
- **Direct Communication:** Engage with your advocates in a personalized manner. Respond to their comments, answer their questions, and thank them for their support. Building relationships builds loyalty.

Encouraging User-Generated Content: Amplify Your Brand Story

User-generated content (UGC) is a powerful tool for building a loyal brand community. When customers create and share content related to your brand, it fosters a sense of authenticity and community. Here are ways to encourage UGC:

- **Host Contests and Giveaways:** Create engaging

contests and giveaways that encourage users to create and share photos, videos, or stories related to your brand.

- **Branded Hashtags:** Develop a unique hashtag for your brand and encourage users to include it in their posts featuring your product or service. This promotes discoverability and allows you to track brand mentions.
- **Interactive Features:** Utilize interactive features like Instagram's Stories or polls to encourage user participation and content creation.
- **User-Generated Content Campaigns:** Develop specific campaigns that incentivise UGC around a particular theme or product launch. This generates excitement and fosters a sense of community involvement.

UGC Guidelines: While encouraging UGC, establish clear guidelines. Outline what type of content is acceptable, and ensure it aligns with your brand values.

Building Brand Loyalty through Social Listening: A Listening Ear

Social media offers a unique opportunity to listen to your audience in real-time. Here's how social listening can build stronger customer relationships and brand loyalty:

- **Track Brand Mentions:** Utilize social listening tools to track mentions of your brand across various platforms. This allows you to identify customer feedback, both positive and negative.
- **Respond Promptly to Concerns:** Don't shy away from negative comments or complaints. Address concerns promptly, professionally, and offer solutions where possible. Addressing negativity head-on demonstrates your commitment to customer satisfaction and prevents issues from escalating.
- **Show Appreciation for Positive Feedback:** Actively acknowledge positive comments and feedback. Thank your customers for their support and show them you value their opinion.

- **Gather Customer Insights:** Analyze social media conversations to understand your audience's needs, preferences, and brand perception. Utilize these insights to refine your marketing strategies and improve your offerings.

Social Listening Tools: Consider investing in social listening tools that offer advanced features like sentiment analysis and competitor tracking. This allows you to gain deeper insights into your brand's social media presence and optimize your overall strategy.

By fostering brand advocacy, encouraging user-generated content, and actively listening to your audience, you build a loyal brand community. This passionate group of supporters becomes the cornerstone of your long-term success in the ever-evolving social media landscape.

CHAPTER 8

ANALYTICS AND MEASURING SUCCESS: DECODING THE DATA FOR SOCIAL MEDIA DOMINATION

In the dynamic world of social media, data is king. By measuring your progress and analyzing key metrics, you can refine your strategies, optimize your campaigns, and achieve your social media goals.

Key Social Media Metrics: The Numbers that Matter

Social media platforms offer a wealth of data and analytics. Here are some fundamental metrics you should focus on to evaluate your social media performance:

- **Reach:** The number of unique users who saw your content. This metric indicates the overall visibility of your social media presence.
- **Engagement:** The level of interaction your content

receives, including likes, comments, shares, clicks, and reactions. High engagement reflects a captivated audience and successful content strategy.

- **Website Traffic:** The number of users who visit your website after clicking on your social media posts. This metric measures the effectiveness of your social media efforts in driving traffic to your website.

- **Conversion Rates:** The percentage of website visitors who take a desired action, such as making a purchase, signing up for a newsletter, or downloading an app. Conversion rates indicate the success of your social media efforts in generating leads and driving sales.

Additional Metrics to Consider: Depending on your specific social media goals, you may also want to track metrics like:

- **Brand Mentions:** The number of times your brand is mentioned on social media, providing insights into brand awareness and sentiment analysis.

- **Follower Growth:** The rate at which your follower base is expanding, indicating the effectiveness of your content and overall reach.
- **Click-Through Rate (CTR):** The percentage of users who click on a link included in your social media post.

Benchmarking: While tracking your own progress is crucial, consider industry benchmarks to understand how your performance stacks up against competitors.

Utilizing Social Media Analytics Tools: Unveiling Hidden Insights

Most social media platforms offer robust built-in analytics tools that provide valuable data on your content performance, audience demographics, and engagement levels. Here's how to leverage these tools effectively:

- **Explore Platform-Specific Analytics:** Familiarize

yourself with the analytics dashboards offered by each platform you use (e.g., Facebook Insights, Twitter Analytics, Instagram Insights). These tools provide insights specific to each platform's functionalities and user behavior.

- **Customize Your Dashboard:** Most analytics tools allow you to personalize your dashboard to focus on the metrics that matter most to your goals. This ensures you're readily accessing the data that informs your social media strategy.
- **Schedule Regular Reporting:** Set up automatic reports to be delivered at regular intervals (e.g., weekly or monthly). This ensures you stay up-to-date on your social media performance and can identify trends over time.

Consider Additional Analytics Software:

For deeper insights and advanced features, consider investing in additional social media analytics software. These tools can offer:

- **Historical Data Comparisons:** Track your progress over time and compare data across different campaigns and content formats.
- **Competitor Analysis:** Benchmark your performance against your competitors and gain insights into their social media strategies.
- **Advanced Reporting Features:** Generate comprehensive reports with detailed data visualizations and actionable recommendations.

Data Visualization is Key: Utilize charts, graphs, and other visual representations to present your data effectively. This simplifies data analysis, identifies trends, and aids in strategy development.

A/B Testing and Optimization: The Continuous Improvement Cycle

Social media is a dynamic landscape, and successful strategies evolve over time. Here's how A/B testing and continuous optimization can take your social media presence to the next level:

- **Run A/B Tests:** Test different variations of your social media strategies by running A/B tests. This could involve comparing different ad copy, posting times, content formats, or visuals.
- **Analyze Data and Refine:** Track the performance of each variation and analyze which ones generate the best results. Based on data insights, refine your strategies and implement winning tactics.
- **Continuous Optimization:** Social media is a continuous learning process. By consistently monitoring your data, testing new approaches, and adapting your strategies, you can optimize your social media presence for maximum impact.

By understanding key metrics, utilizing powerful analytics tools, and implementing A/B testing, you can transform your social media data into actionable insights and continuously optimize your strategies for long-term success.

CHAPTER 9

Staying Ahead of the Curve: Social Media Trends in a Dynamic Landscape

The social media landscape is constantly evolving. New platforms emerge, user behavior shifts, and algorithms change.

Emerging Social Media Platforms: The Next Big Thing?

Social media isn't static; new platforms are constantly vying for user attention. Here's how to stay ahead of the curve:

- **Stay Informed:** Keep yourself updated about emerging social media platforms. Research their target demographics, functionalities, and potential for your brand.

- **Test and Adapt:** Don't be afraid to experiment with new platforms. Allocate a small portion of your resources to test the waters and see if they resonate with your target audience.
- **Focus on Value:** Regardless of the platform, prioritize creating valuable content tailored to the specific audience and functionalities of the platform.

Remember: Not every new platform will be a perfect fit for your brand. Be strategic in your approach and focus on platforms with the potential to reach your target audience effectively.

The Rise of Social Commerce: Shopping Made Easy

Social commerce is transforming the way we shop. Here's how to leverage this growing trend:

- **Shoppable Posts and Features:** Utilize built-in features like shoppable posts on Instagram or Facebook to showcase products and enable direct purchasing within the platform.

- **Live Streaming Commerce:** Explore live streaming features to demonstrate products, answer customer questions, and create a more interactive shopping experience.

- **Influencer Marketing Partnerships:** Collaborate with social media influencers to promote your products and leverage their audience reach to drive sales.

Social Commerce Requires Optimization: Ensure your social media profiles are optimized for social commerce. Include clear product descriptions, high-quality visuals, and easy-to-follow purchase processes.

Future-Proofing Your Social Media Strategy: A Long-Term Vision

The key to social media success lies in adapting to change. Here's how to future-proof your strategy:

- **Stay Informed About Algorithm Changes:** Social media platforms constantly update their algorithms. Stay informed about these changes and adapt your content strategy accordingly to ensure maximum reach and engagement.

- **Explore New Advertising Options:** New advertising options and targeting functionalities emerge regularly. Research and experiment with these options to reach your target audience more effectively.

- **Focus on User Behavior:** User behavior on social media evolves over time. Conduct ongoing research and analysis to understand how your audience interacts with content and adapt your strategy accordingly.

Embrace Continuous Learning: The world of social media is dynamic. Embrace lifelong learning, stay curious about new trends, and continuously refine your approach to ensure your social media presence remains relevant and impactful in the years to come.

By implementing the strategies outlined in this book, understanding key metrics, and staying informed about evolving trends, you can harness the power of social media to achieve your marketing goals and build a thriving online community for your brand.

CHAPTER 10

Conclusion: Mastering Social Media - A Journey of Dedication and Continuous Growth

Social media marketing isn't a magic bullet; it's a strategic journey that requires dedication, consistent effort, and a willingness to learn and adapt. This concluding chapter emphasizes the importance of perseverance, celebrating your wins, and embracing the ever-evolving social media landscape.

The Importance of Consistency: Building Momentum for Long-Term Success

Think of social media marketing as a marathon, not a sprint. Consistent effort is key to building a thriving online presence and achieving your marketing goals. Here's why consistency is crucial:

- **Building Relationships:** Social media is about fostering connections with your audience. Consistent posting and engagement allow you to build rapport, establish trust, and keep your brand top-of-mind.

- **Maintaining Visibility:** Disappearing acts don't win on social media. Regular posting ensures you stay visible in your audience's feeds and keeps your brand relevant in their minds.

- **Data-Driven Optimization:** Consistency allows you to gather valuable data over time. By analyzing trends in engagement, reach, and conversions, you can continually optimize your strategies for maximum impact.

Develop a Content Calendar: Planning your content in advance ensures consistency and streamlines your workflow. Create a content calendar to schedule posts, diversify content types, and maintain a steady stream of engaging content for your audience.

Celebrate Your Wins and Learn from Losses: Tracking Progress for Informed Decisions

Social media marketing is a journey of learning and growth. Here's how tracking your progress and analyzing results can fuel your success:

- **Celebrate Milestones:** Reaching a follower milestone, achieving a high engagement rate, or exceeding a sales target are all reasons to celebrate! Acknowledge your achievements and recognize your hard work.
- **Analyze Performance Data:** Don't just post and pray. Regularly analyze key metrics like reach, engagement, and conversions to understand what content resonates with your audience and what needs improvement.
- **Learn from What Doesn't Work:** Not every post will be a home run. Analyze content that underperformed and identify areas for improvement. Adapt your strategies based on data insights.

Embrace a Growth Mindset: View challenges as opportunities to learn and grow. The social media landscape is dynamic, and there will be setbacks along the way. Embrace a growth mindset, continuously learn, and adapt your strategies for continued success.

Embrace the Journey: The Evolving World of Social Media

The world of social media is like a living organism, constantly evolving and changing. Here's why staying informed and adaptable is crucial:

- **Emerging Trends:** New platforms, features, and user behaviors emerge all the time. Staying informed about these trends allows you to capitalize on new opportunities and reach your target audience effectively.
- **Algorithm Updates:** Social media platforms regularly update their algorithms, impacting how content is displayed in user feeds. Stay informed

about these changes and adapt your content strategy accordingly.

- **Lifelong Learning:** The key to staying ahead in social media marketing is continuous learning. Read industry publications, attend workshops, and stay curious about new trends and best practices.

Social Media is a Journey, Not a Destination: Embrace the ever-evolving nature of social media. Be prepared to experiment with different strategies, adapt to new trends, and continuously learn to ensure your social media presence remains relevant and impactful in the years to come.

By implementing the strategies outlined in this comprehensive guide, consistently creating valuable content, and embracing the journey of continuous learning, you can master the art of social media marketing and achieve remarkable success in the ever-evolving digital landscape.

Bonus Chapter

Social Media Management Tools and Resources - Your All-in-One Toolkit for Success

Mastering social media marketing requires the right tools and resources at your fingertips. This bonus chapter equips you with a comprehensive list of popular platforms and websites to streamline your workflow, enhance your content creation, and gain valuable insights from your social media presence.

Social Media Management Tools:

- **Buffer:** A user-friendly platform for scheduling posts across various social media platforms, analyzing performance, and engaging with your audience.
- **Hootsuite:** A robust platform for managing multiple

social media accounts, scheduling content, monitoring brand mentions, and running social media advertising campaigns.

- **Sprout Social:** An all-in-one solution offering scheduling, engagement, analytics, and social listening capabilities, ideal for agencies and larger businesses.
- **SocialPilot:** A budget-friendly option for scheduling posts, managing multiple accounts, and generating basic social media reports.
- **Later:** Primarily focused on Instagram marketing, Later offers scheduling, content creation tools, and analytics specifically designed for the visual platform.

Choosing the Right Tool: Consider your needs, budget, and team size when selecting a social media management tool. Many platforms offer free plans with limited features, while premium plans offer advanced functionalities.

Design Resources:

- **Canva:** A user-friendly online design platform with pre-made templates, stock photos, and design elements to create stunning social media graphics, presentations, and infographics, even for those without design experience.
- **Piktochart:** Another user-friendly design platform offering infographic templates, social media graphics, and presentations with a focus on data visualization.
- **Adobe Creative Suite:** Industry-standard design software like Photoshop and Illustrator for professional-grade image editing, graphic design, and video creation (paid subscription required).

Free Design Resources: Numerous websites offer free stock photos, icons, and design elements, such as:

- **Unsplash**
- **Pexels**

- **Freepik**

Stock Photo and Video Websites:

- **Shutterstock:** A vast library of high-quality royalty-free stock photos, videos, and music for professional use (paid subscription or per-item purchase).
- **Adobe Stock:** Another extensive collection of royalty-free stock photos, videos, illustrations, and design templates integrated with Adobe Creative Suite (paid subscription).
- **Getty Images:** A premium stock photo and video website with a curated selection of high-resolution images and footage (paid subscription or per-item purchase).

Free Stock Photo and Video Resources: While the selection may be more limited, some websites offer free stock photos and videos for commercial use, such as:

- **Pexels Videos**
- **Pixabay**
- **Videvo**

Social Listening Platforms:

- **Brand24:** A social listening platform for tracking brand mentions, analyzing sentiment, and engaging with your audience across various social media channels.
- **Sprout Social Listening:** A feature within the Sprout Social platform that allows you to monitor brand mentions, analyze competitor activity, and gain insights into audience sentiment.
- **Hootsuite Brandwatch:** A powerful social listening tool integrated with Hootsuite, offering comprehensive brand monitoring, competitor analysis, and social media analytics.

Free Social Listening Tools: While functionalities might be limited, some free tools can offer basic brand monitoring capabilities:

- **Mention**
- **Tweetdeck** (for monitoring Twitter mentions)

Remember: This list is not exhaustive, and new tools and resources emerge constantly. Research and explore different options to find the ones that best suit your specific needs and budget.

By leveraging the power of social media management tools, design resources, stock media websites, and social listening platforms, you can streamline your workflow, create high-quality content, gain valuable insights from your audience, and ultimately achieve remarkable success in your social media marketing endeavors.

ABOUT THE AUTHOR

Riley Anderson is a multifaceted individual, blending the roles of business guru, writer, and motivational speaker. With a keen insight into the intricacies of publishing and a talent for inspiring others, Riley has become a sought-after figure in both the literary and entrepreneurial worlds.

In terms of education, Riley holds a degree in Business Administration with a focus on Marketing from a reputable university. This educational background, coupled with years of practical experience, has equipped Riley with the knowledge and skills needed to navigate the competitive landscape of both the business and publishing industries. Whether through written works or captivating speeches, Riley's aim is to empower and guide individuals on their journey to success.

www.ingramcontent.com/pod-product-compliance
Lightning Source LLC
Chambersburg PA
CBHW050238230526
45470CB00005B/2009